SUPERSTARS
2013

BY K. C. KELLEY

SCHOLASTIC INC.

Photo credits:

Front cover, top left: MSA/Icon SMI/Corbis; front cover, top right: Hannah Foslien/Getty Images; front cover, bottom left: Rich Gabrielson/Icon SMI/Corbis; front cover, bottom right: Evan Pinkus/AP Images; back cover, left: Andrew Richardson/Icon SMI/Corbis; back cover, center: Don Kelly/Corbis; back cover, right: G. Newman Lowrance/AP Images; p5: Jared Wickerham/Getty Images; p7: Chris Szagola/Cal Sport Media/Corbis; p9: Icon SMI/Corbis; p11: MSA/Icon SMI/Corbis; p13: David Drapkin/AP Images; p15: Joe Mahoney/AP Images; p17: Tom DiPace/AP Images; p19: Jeff Lewis/Icon SMI/Corbis; p21: Aaron M. Sprecher/AP Images; p23: Andrew Richardson/Icon SMI/Corbis; p25: Todd Kirkland/Icon SMI/Corbis; p27: Chris Szagola/ZUMA Press/Corbis; p29: Scott Boehm/AP Images; p31: Kevin Terrell/AP Images; p32: John G. Mabanglo/EPA/Newscom.

ISBN 978-0-545-58515-6

12 11 10 9 8 7 6 5 4 3 2 1   13 14 15 16 17 18/0

Printed in the U.S.A.   40
First printing, September 2013

Cover designed by Cheung Tai
Interior designed by Heather Barber
Photo editor: Cynthia Carris

CONTENTS

TOM BRADY
QUARTERBACK, NEW ENGLAND PATRIOTS

When the right chance to succeed comes along, you have to grab it. You might never have another shot. In 2000, Tom Brady got his chance . . . and has since become one of the greatest quarterbacks of all time.

Brady was a sixth-round draft pick out of Michigan. He was the second-string quarterback in New England behind superstar Drew Bledsoe. But an injury to Bledsoe sent Brady scrambling for his helmet! Brady showed the Patriots and the NFL that he was no late-round pick. In his second season, he led New England to its first Super Bowl win. Then he carried them to two more titles in the next three years, taking home MVP in two of his Super Bowl wins.

Brady is at his best in the big games. He has become legendary for his ability to come from behind to win. In two of the Pats' Super Bowl victories, he steered them on drives, leading to game-winning field goals. He has a great arm, of course, and can run a little. But it's his calm, cool leadership that is his greatest strength. In 2012, Brady became the first NFL quarterback to take his team to ten straight division championships. Nothing ever seems to bother him. Brady seems happiest when his team is down, the clock is ticking, the opposing team's fans are screaming . . . and he has the ball.

BRADY FILE

Rookie Season	2000
Years in League	13
Pass Attempts	5,958
Completions	3,798
Touchdowns	334
Passing Yards	44,806
Interceptions Thrown	123
Passer Rating	96.6

6'4", 225 lbs
University of Michigan
Sixth round–2000 by Patriots

- NFL record 50 TD passes in 2007
- Named to eight Pro Bowl teams
- Third all-time in passer rating

❝I think . . . I've got it all figured out. There's nothing that can shock me anymore. There's nothing I haven't anticipated . . . there is a calmness [to how I play].❞

ARIAN FOSTER
RUNNING BACK, HOUSTON TEXANS

Over and over again in his football career, Arian Foster was overlooked. He didn't make his high-school team the first two times he tried out. In college, he was second-string for two years. Then an injury sent NFL scouts running. He was not even drafted!

But after fighting his way into a starting spot for the Texans in 2010, Foster made sure no one will ever overlook him again. In his first season as a starter, he led the NFL with 1,616 rushing yards and 16 scores on the ground. In 2012, he led the league with 351 carries and 15 rushing TDs.

Foster's running style is like the poetry that he likes to write: smooth and powerful. He is not a back who will bury his head into the line. Rather, he's an expert at finding the smallest gap and slipping through. Once clear, he has the speed to outrun all defenders. He can also catch the ball, averaging more than 40 receptions a year.

With Foster pushing the ground game and QB Matt Schaub improving as a passer, the Texans have become one of the NFL's best all-around teams. Just like their star runner, no one will overlook them again.

FOSTER FILE

Rookie Season	2009
Years in League	4
Rushing Attempts	1,010
Rushing Yards	4,521
Rushing Touchdowns	44
Receptions	167
Receiving Yards	1,531
Receiving Touchdowns	6

6'1", 229 lbs
University of Tennessee
Undrafted free agent–signed
2009 by Texans

- Set Texans' team record with 231 yards in a 2010 game against the Indianapolis Colts
- Named to three Pro Bowl teams
- Led NFL in total touchdowns in 2010 with 18

"This league is all about opportunities. I came in, low status, worked my way up, and this is my time to help this team."

A. J. GREEN
WIDE RECEIVER, CINCINNATI BENGALS

How's this for a great start? In his first NFL game, A. J. Green caught a 41-yard touchdown pass that gave the Bengals a win over the Cleveland Browns. It was the start of something big. Green led all NFL rookies in receptions and yards in 2011. He continued his game-breaking success in 2012, with 97 catches for 1,350 yards and 11 touchdowns. He also earned his second Pro Bowl selection—the way he's going, there will be many more.

While playing for Summerville High School in South Carolina, Green was considered one of the best receivers in the country. When he moved on to the University of Georgia, he kept setting records. He led the SEC in receiving yards as a freshman, breaking every school record along the way. Over his next two seasons, he was one of college football's deep-threat stars.

Joining the Bengals as a first-round draft pick, Green teamed with fellow rookie Andy Dalton. Few rookie QB-WR duos have ever been as successful. When Green caught 10 passes versus the Broncos, it was the most by a rookie . . . thrown by a rookie! The Dalton-to-Green combination was responsible for the Bengals making the playoffs. In 2012, they made the playoffs again, as Green moved into the elite of NFL wideouts.

GREEN FILE

Rookie Season	2011
Years in League	2
Receptions	162
Receiving Yards	2,407
Receiving Touchdowns	18

6'4", 207 lbs
University of Georgia
First round–2011 by Bengals

- A. J. stands for Adriel Jeremiah
- Credits juggling lessons for helping his hand-eye coordination
- His 5,373 high-school career receiving yards is ranked second all-time

" It's only the beginning; I can't wait to see what I will have accomplished over the next ten years. "

CALVIN JOHNSON
WIDE RECEIVER, DETROIT LIONS

Greatest nickname in the NFL? That's easy. Megatron.

Best wide receiver in the NFL? Also easy, and same answer.

Detroit's Calvin Johnson was a very good NFL wide receiver for his first four seasons, leading the NFL in receiving touchdowns in 2008 and topping 60 catches three times. But in 2011 and 2012, he truly earned his awesome nickname. In 2011, he led the NFL with 1,681 receiving yards while setting career highs with sixteen TDs and 96 catches. Fantasy-football players were almost as excited as Lions fans to watch this superstar emerge.

In 2012, however, Megatron truly transformed into a legend. In Detroit's fifteenth game, he broke Jerry Rice's record for most receiving yards in a season. Rice had 1,848 in 1995. Johnson set the new mark at 1,964 yards. He also led the NFL with 122 receptions.

Even when the opposing team knows the ball is going his way, Megatron finds a way to make the catch. He can snag balls one-handed by leaping above defenders, or by diving for low throws. Few players have ever combined his size and strength with such soft hands. Armor up, NFL defenses: Megatron is coming back for more!

JOHNSON FILE

Rookie Season	2007
Years in League	6
Receptions	488
Receiving Yards	7,836
Receiving Touchdowns	54

6'5", 236 lbs
Georgia Institute of Technology
First round–2007 by Lions

- Two-time first-team All-Pro
- Chosen as cover subject of *Madden 13* video game
- 2006 All-American and ACC Player of the Year

It's a huge accomplishment to take one of those records from the great Jerry. All the work that we put in this year, I guess you can say it's well deserved.

MARSHAWN LYNCH
RUNNING BACK, SEATTLE SEAHAWKS

Suiting up for an NFL game, the mild-mannered Marshawn Lynch undergoes a change. He switches from everyday life into "Beast Mode" and transforms into one of the NFL's most powerful running backs.

The Buffalo Bills nabbed him with their first-round pick in 2007. He had several solid seasons with Buffalo, twice topping 1,000 rushing yards. Midway through the 2010 season, however, the Bills traded Lynch to the Seahawks. Lynch hoped for a fresh start in Seattle, but spent the rest of 2010 splitting time with Justin Forsett. His 67-yard TD run in a 2010 playoff game—complete with a famous stiff-arm—hinted at great things to come.

In 2011, Seattle turned its rushing offense over to Lynch and he delivered. Beast Mode set career highs with 12 touchdowns and 1,204 yards. His bruising style was a perfect fit for coach Pete Carroll's offense.

But 2011 was just a preview. In 2012, after superstar rookie quarterback Russell Wilson joined the team, Lynch moved into the elite class of NFL runners. His 1,590 rushing yards were third in the NFL and he helped spark Seattle to a division title and a playoff spot. Though they fell short to the Atlanta Falcons, the Seahawks are a team on the rise. And with players like Lynch, that rise is almost sure to continue.

LYNCH FILE

Rookie Season	2007
Years in League	6
Rushing Attempts	1,452
Rushing Yards	6,132
Rushing Touchdowns	46
Receptions	166
Receiving Yards	1,216
Receiving Touchdowns	3

5'11", 215 lbs
University of California, Berkeley
First round–2007 by Bills

- Nicknamed "Man-Child" by coach of his Pop Warner team, the Oakland Dynamites
- Named to three Pro Bowl teams
- Threw a halfback-option TD pass in 2007

" We just love to play hard-nosed football. "

PEYTON MANNING
QUARTERBACK, DENVER BRONCOS

Peyton Manning joined the Indianapolis Colts in 1998 and turned them into winners. He led his team to eleven 10-win seasons, including a victory in Super Bowl XLI. His ability to read defenses and call plays at the line sets him apart from most other signal-callers. Add to that a powerful arm and a granite will and you've got a recipe for a winner. After setting tons of passing records and establishing himself as one of the best ever, did he have more to prove? The answer is yes.

After a neck injury forced Manning to miss the entire 2011 season, some experts thought his Hall of Fame career was over. He felt otherwise. Moving to the Denver Broncos in 2012, Manning struggled early on. The team lost three of its first six games. But then Manning got the team on the same page. They won their last eleven games of the regular season and roared into the playoffs with the AFC's best record. A highlight was coming back from being behind 24–0 at halftime against the San Diego Chargers. In the end, Manning led the NFL with 37 TD passes and made his twelfth Pro Bowl, proving that he was still one of the game's best.

MANNING FILE

Rookie Season	1998
Years in League	15
Pass Attempts	7,793
Completions	5,082
Touchdowns	436
Passing Yards	59,487
Interceptions Thrown	252
Passer Rating	95.7

6'5", 230 lbs
University of Tennessee
First round–1998 by Colts

- Set NFL record with 49 TD passes in 2004 (topped by Brady's 50 in 2007)

- Only player with four NFL MVP awards (2003, 2004, 2008, 2009)

- Father Archie was an NFL QB; brother Eli is QB for the New York Giants

Knowing I don't have fifteen years left to play football, there is a sense of urgency to win championships.

Doug Martin was Tampa Bay's first pick in the 2012 draft, but he wasn't slated to start. Through the team's first seven games, he split time with LaGarrette Blount. That ended for good after his amazing game against the Oakland Raiders on November 4. Martin ran for four touchdowns and a team-record 251 yards. Three of those scores were for 40 or more yards (45, 67, and 70). He joins Mike Anderson (in 2000) as the only players ever with 250-plus yards and a quartet of TDs. In December, NFL.com named Martin's Oakland performance as the Best Single-Game Performance of the Year.

He had his big day in a familiar city. Martin had grown up in Oakland before going to high school in Stockton, California. He played college ball at Boise State, where he scored 43 touchdowns in three seasons as a starter.

Martin is only 5'9", short for a football player, but he makes up for it with strength and speed. He doesn't like it, but his talents earned him a unique nickname: the Muscle Hamster.

MARTIN FILE

Rookie Season	2012
Years in League	1
Rushing Attempts	319
Rushing Yards	1,454
Rushing Touchdowns	11
Receptions	49
Receiving Yards	472
Receiving Touchdowns	1

5'9", 223 lbs
Boise State University
First round–2012 by Buccaneers

- Had four games with 125 or more yards
- Finished second in the NFL in yards from scrimmage
- Was Offensive Rookie of the Month in October 2012

❝Muscle Hamster has to be the worst nickname ever. It started back in college, but I just can't shake it.❞

ADRIAN PETERSON
RUNNING BACK, MINNESOTA VIKINGS

When Adrian Peterson was injured on Christmas Eve 2011, most experts wrote off his 2012 season. His knee injury was so serious that he had to have surgery. Other players with similar injuries needed more than a year to recover.

But Peterson was back on the field for the Vikings' opening game in 2012. His speedy recovery is almost as amazing as his superb career. Peterson had scored 10 or more rushing TDs in each of his first five seasons and was the rushing champion in 2008. So a dominating Adrian Peterson was not a surprise.

What was a surprise was that he got even better after his injury. Peterson missed the all-time single-season rushing record by only nine yards! He finished with 2,097 yards. That was the second most in a season, and only the seventh time that a player has topped 2,000 yards. He had 11 touchdowns to keep his double-digit score streak going.

He was humble about his comeback and, thanks to his domination, the Vikings were in the hunt for a playoff spot until the last game of the season.

One of Peterson's nicknames is "All Day," but after his 2012 performance, you can change that to "All Time."

PETERSON FILE

Rookie Season	2007
Years in League	6
Rushing Attempts	1,754
Rushing Yards	8,849
Rushing Touchdowns	76
Receptions	177
Receiving Yards	1,526
Receiving Touchdowns	4

6'1", 217 lbs
University of Oklahoma
First round–2007 by Vikings

- Led NFL with 18 touchdowns in 2009
- Named to five Pro Bowl teams
- Finished second in 2004 Heisman Trophy voting as a freshman

My main motivation [for coming back] was greatness, because in my heart I want to be the best to have ever played. So, coming back from this injury, I had to fight through that to do that.

TROY POLAMALU
SAFETY, PITTSBURGH STEELERS

With his long, curly hair spilling out of his black Steelers helmet, Troy Polamalu is easy to spot on a football field. Opposing teams know that they have to avoid him at all costs. Polamalu's tough play and leadership were key to the Steelers' two Super Bowl wins in 2006 and 2008. The way he plays his position is unique: He lines up wherever he thinks the play will be. Polamalu gets more freedom to operate than most players, thanks to the trust his coaches have in his talent and experience.

After playing several sports as a kid growing up in Oregon, Polamalu focused on football at the University of Southern California. His college success led to the Steelers taking him with their first draft pick in 2003. Pittsburgh has a long tradition of hard-hitting defenders, and Polamalu fit right in. He made the Pro Bowl in his second season and has been the best strong safety in the NFL ever since.

In 2009, he missed eleven games due to injury, and the Steelers didn't make the playoffs. The same thing happened in 2012, when Polamalu missed seven games. That just shows how important Polamalu is to Pittsburgh. He should be back and healthy in 2013, which is bad news for Steelers' opponents . . . and great news for Pittsburgh fans.

POLAMALU FILE

Rookie Season	2003
Years in League	10
Tackles	487
Interceptions	30
Fumbles Recovered	5
Sacks	10
Touchdowns	2

5'10", 213 lbs
University of
Southern California
First round—2003 by Steelers

- Named to seven Pro Bowl teams
- Two-time first-team All American at USC
- All-state in high school for baseball as a centerfielder

"Throughout history, every great warrior—the Greeks, the Samurais, the American Indians, the Mongolians, you name it—had long hair and would dress it before battle."

RAY RICE
RUNNING BACK, BALTIMORE RAVENS

Few running backs have ever combined pass-catching ability with breakaway speed and powerful up-the-middle running. With all those skills, Ray Rice is probably the best all-around back in the NFL today. He has finished in the top three in yards from scrimmage three times, twice topping 2,000 yards. He has had at least 60 catches for 475 yards in every season he has been a starter for Baltimore.

Rice first showed his all-around skills at Rutgers University. The school had not been doing well, but Rice changed all that. In 2005, his first season there, Rutgers had a winning record for the first time since 1992. In 2006, Rutgers won its first bowl game ever. Rice set a school record that year with 1,794 yards. After another great year as a junior in 2007, Rice headed to the NFL, where the Ravens snapped him up in the second round.

While it takes a lot of talent to do all those things well, it also takes mental toughness. He has to adjust his mind-set to be a power runner, a pass catcher, or a speed merchant. With an average of 1,250 yards over four straight seasons, Rice has the running game down pat. He has at least one receiving TD each year, too. He even threw a touchdown pass in 2011!

RICE FILE

Rookie Season	2008
Years in League	5
Rushing Attempts	1,216
Rushing Yards	5,520
Rushing Touchdowns	33
Receptions	311
Receiving Yards	2,713
Receiving Touchdowns	6

5'9", 195 lbs
Rutgers University
Second round–2008 by Ravens

- Led NFL with 2,068 yards from scrimmage in 2011
- One of only two players with more than 1,200 rushing and 700 receiving yards in two seasons (2009 and 2011)
- Won state championship with New Rochelle High School in New York

"I was taught that I cannot back down to anything. I was trained never to be scared."

MATT RYAN
QUARTERBACK, ATLANTA FALCONS

Matt Ryan has led the Falcons for five seasons, stepping into the starting quarterback role as a rookie in 2008. He has topped the league in one major passing stat (completion percentage in 2012). He has made it to only one Pro Bowl. So why is he a superstar?

The answer is in the standings. Since Ryan took over, the Falcons have never had a losing record. They have won at least ten games in all but one of his five seasons in charge. Simply put: Ryan is a winner.

Atlanta won only four games in 2007. They used their first-round pick, the third overall, to choose Ryan. In his senior year at Boston College, Ryan was named the ACC player of the year and won the Johnny Unitas Award, given to the nation's top QB. Atlanta handed him the starting job as a rookie, in part for his passing skill but also for his great leadership. How much of a leader is he? In high school, he was captain of his school's football, basketball, and baseball teams.

Good call, Falcons. Ryan's first pass as a pro went for a 62-yard score. By his second season, his teammates had made him co-captain. Ryan's ability to rally his team helped the Falcons to one of the best runs in franchise history. They have made the playoffs in four seasons. In 2012, they made it to the NFC Championship game.

RYAN FILE

Rookie Season	2008
Years in League	5
Pass Attempts	2,637
Completions	1,654
Touchdowns	127
Passing Yards	18,957
Interceptions Thrown	60
Passer Rating	90.9

6'4", 220 lbs
Boston College
First round–2008 by Falcons

- Was the 2008 Offensive Rookie of the Year
- Met his wife, Sarah, at Boston College where she played basketball
- Led NFL with five fourth-quarter comebacks in 2010 and 2012

❝I want to be around here a long time, with this team, go to the playoffs and hopefully win a championship.❞

ALDON SMITH
LINEBACKER, SAN FRANCISCO 49ERS

No pass rusher in NFL history has had so much success as fast as Aldon Smith. The powerful speed linebacker had 33.5 sacks in his first two seasons. That broke the NFL record held by Hall of Famer Reggie White. Smith also reached 30 sacks for his career in just thirty-seven games, faster than any other player.

Smith was all over the news as a rookie. He was twice named the Defensive Rookie of the Month. On November 19, 2011, he had 5.5 sacks against the Chicago Bears. That was the most ever on Monday Night Football (and they've been playing that night for forty-two years!). His season total of 14 was the most among rookies and just a half sack shy of the NFL record.

With his success as a rookie, Smith should have been no surprise for teams in 2012, but somehow he managed to improve even more. His 19.5 sacks are in the top-ten ranking of the most ever by a player in a single season. That total was also the most ever by a 49er.

In high school, along with being a basketball star, Smith was considered one of the best high-school defensive football players in the nation. At the University of Missouri, he was on many all-conference and all-star teams while playing defensive end. The Niners made him their first pick in 2011 and moved him to linebacker. So far, no one has been able to stop him.

SMITH FILE

Rookie Season	2011
Years in League	2
Sacks	33.5
Interceptions	1
Fumbles Recovered	1

6'4", 263 lbs
University of Missouri
First round–2011 by 49ers

- Pro Football Writers Association Defensive Rookie of the Year in 2011
- Snagged first career interception in big win over Patriots in 2012 playoffs
- Does boxing and martial-arts training to improve pass-rush skills

" [My sacks in 2012 were] definitely a good achievement, setting the franchise record . . . It means a lot to me . . . [but I have to] keep it going and see if I can make that number even better."

JASON PIERRE-PAUL
DEFENSIVE END, NEW YORK GIANTS

The quarterback-sacking machine known as JPP got a late start on football. Pierre-Paul grew up in southern Florida, playing basketball. His parents, who had moved to Florida from Haiti, didn't want him to play football because they thought it was too rough. However, Pierre-Paul's folks said yes when he was a junior. That year, he helped his high school's football team reach the title game.

After high school, top colleges wanted him, but his grades were not good enough . . . yet. Pierre-Paul knew he needed experience on the field and growth in the classroom. After two years in junior college—one in California and one in Kansas—he was ready. At the University of South Florida, he had a huge impact and was named All-American. Next stop: the NFL.

After a rookie season spent learning more about the game, he had a breakout second year. His talents were on full display in a big win over the Cowboys. After a sack, a forced fumble, and a safety, he blocked what would have been the game-tying field goal. On the season, he had 16.5 sacks and went to his first Pro Bowl. More importantly, he was part of a defense that bottled up the Patriots to win Super Bowl XLVI. In 2012, Jason's sack numbers were down a bit, but he did have his first NFL interception. He made it a big one, returning it for a touchdown against the Cowboys.

PIERRE-PAUL FILE

Rookie Season	2010
Years in League	3
Sacks	27.5
Interceptions	1
Fumbles Recovered	3

6'5", 278 lbs
University of South Florida
First round–2010 by Giants

- Coaches say his nonstop hustle is his greatest football gift
- Named All-American in only season at USF
- Got first career interception and TD in win over Dallas in 2012

❝However many snaps I play for, when I'm on the field, I go 120 percent.❞

REGGIE WAYNE
WIDE RECEIVER, INDIANAPOLIS COLTS

For the first half of his career, Reggie Wayne was not the main option in Indianapolis. Marvin Harrison was the top receiver teaming up with quarterback Peyton Manning in the Colts' high-power passing offense. Wayne was the number-two pass catcher. He had some great seasons, including 12 TDs in 2004 and three 1,000-yard seasons. But he was not "the man."

Harrison was hurt in 2007, however, and Wayne emerged as a superstar. Manning connected with his number two as well as he had done with his number one—Wayne led the NFL with 1,510 receiving yards. Harrison retired in 2008, and Wayne has been the top pass catcher in Indy ever since.

In 2012, his veteran skills helped rookie quarterback Andrew Luck settle in quickly. Wayne put up the second-highest yardage total of his career. No one has more catches in the NFL since 2004 than Wayne (718). And he also moved into the top-ten all-time in receptions, with 968 through 2012.

Wayne isn't the biggest receiver, often standing several inches shorter than the safeties who cover him. However, he has always run perfect routes. Add in speed and sure hands and you've got a player that Luck and the Colts can depend on. And talk about dependable: Wayne has missed only one game in the past ten seasons!

WAYNE FILE

Rookie Season	2001
Years in League	12
Receptions	968
Receiving Yards	13,063
Receiving Touchdowns	78

6'0", 198 lbs
University of Miami
First round–2001 by Colts

- Fifth player ever with four 100-catch seasons
- Set all-time receptions record in college (173)
- Named to six Pro Bowl teams

> The name of the game is longevity. I know to get longevity, you need to be in shape, you need to [be] healthy, you need to get in that weight room and do what you need to do.

2012 NFL STANDINGS

AFC EAST		AFC NORTH		AFC SOUTH		AFC WEST	
Patriots	12–4	Ravens	10–6	Texans	12–4	Broncos	13–3
Dolphins	7–9	Bengals	10–6	Colts	11–5	Chargers	7–9
Jets	6–10	Steelers	8–8	Titans	6–10	Raiders	4–12
Bills	6–10	Browns	5–11	Jaguars	2–14	Chiefs	2–14

NFC EAST		NFC NORTH		NFC SOUTH		NFC WEST	
Redskins	10–6	Packers	11–5	Falcons	13–3	49ers	11–4–1
Giants	9–7	Vikings	10–6	Panthers	7–9	Seahawks	11–5
Cowboys	8–8	Bears	10–6	Saints	7–9	Rams	7–8–1
Eagles	4–12	Lions	4–12	Buccaneers	7–9	Cardinals	5–11

SUPER BOWL XLVII, NEW ORLEANS
Ravens 34, 49ers 31